BIBLE ACTIVITIES IN A SNAP

Sharing God's Love

Written and Illustrated by Barbara Rodgers

Rainbow Books

Rainbow Publishers • P.O. Box 261129 • San Diego, CA 92196

To Lorraine, my friend, mentor and sister in Christ:
thanks for all of the encouragement.

BIBLE ACTIVITIES IN A SNAP, SHARING GOD'S LOVE
©2001 by Rainbow Publishers, fourth printing
ISBN 1-885358-45-8

Rainbow Publishers
P.O. Box 261129
San Diego, CA 92196

Author and Illustrator: Barbara Rodgers
Editor: Christy Allen
Cover Design: Stray Cat Studio, San Diego, CA

Scriptures are from the *Holy Bible: New International Version*
(North American Edition), copyright ©1973, 1978, 1984
by the International Bible Society. Used by permission of
Zondervan Bible Publishers.

Printed in the United States of America

Contents

Introduction

Welcome to *Bible Activities in a Snap*, a unique book series intended to bring joy, satisfaction and biblical understanding to children ages 3-8. Sunday School teachers, children's church leaders, Christian school teachers and home school parents will find this book series helpful for:

• reinforcing Bible lessons

• teaching spiritual concepts and biblical truths

• inspiring children's creativity

• providing lesson extension materials

This exciting concept offers two pages per lesson. For younger or less-skilled students, the left-hand page offers a finished illustration ready to color. The right-hand page of the same lesson is partially illustrated, allowing older or advanced children to use their imaginations and complete the scene. And because the pages are reproducible, you can duplicate the sheets to expand your curriculum, then allow the children to select the activity level they prefer. Every page includes a short narration and Scripture verse, so *Bible Activities in a Snap* may complement a lesson or serve as lessons themselves, making preparation truly a snap!

Here are some tips to get the best results from *Bible Activities in a Snap*:

• The pages are perforated for easy tear-out. However, you may want to copy them directly from the book to keep the lessons organized.

• When photocopying a page, place a sheet of black construction paper on the back of the original so the copier will not duplicate any print from the reverse side.

• Try offering different media for coloring, such as crayons of all shapes and colors, markers, colored pencils, chalk, paint and glitter pens.

• Show how to enhance some of the pictures by gluing basic elements to them such as yellow yarn for straw or cotton balls for sheep.

• Give the children additional instructions for drawing on the illustrations, or challenge the kids to devise their own one-of-a-kind work. There is no limit to the teaching and learning possibilities!

• Consider using the sheets as take-home pages for parental review so families may reinforce the lessons at home.

These books are so easy to duplicate and use that your only requirement is the desire to touch the hearts of young children with God's Word. Watch your children grow spiritually as God's precious Word is impressed upon their hearts and minds knowing "that your labor in the Lord is not in vain." (1 Corinthians 15:58)

Valentine's Day

Valentine's Day is a great time to share the love of Christ by doing kind things for people. The simple act of sending people valentines and letting them know that you love them and God loves them is one way. Draw flowers in the bouquet of leaves in the vase on the opposite page and give the sheet to someone for Valentine's Day.

Dear friends, let us love one another, for love comes from God. 1 John 4:7

TO: _____

FROM: _____

This Valentine wish
is full of love,
That only God gives
us from above.

Wishing you a Jesus-filled Valentine's Day!

This is how God showed his love among us:
He sent his one and only Son into the world that we might live through him. 1 John 4:9

Basket of Hearts

Have you ever made cookies to give away to express your love or care toward others? We show people the love of Jesus when we do little acts of kindness. Sending cards or letters is one great way to do this. Can you think of someone to whom you could send a valentine? On the opposite page, draw hearts inside the basket that the puppy is holding, then give the sheet to a special friend.

Dear friends, since God so loved us, we also ought to love one another. 1 John 4:11

8

This basket of love
Comes along your way
To wish you the best
On this Valentine's Day!

TO: _____

FROM: _____

Love one another deeply, from the heart. 1 Peter 1:22

Celebrate Easter

When we celebrate Easter, we celebrate the resurrection of Jesus Christ, our Lord. Many people do not know the real reason why we celebrate Easter. They may only celebrate it with Spring flowers, candy treats and Easter eggs. But we know that Easter gives us the hope of eternal life through Jesus. You can share what Easter is all about with someone who does not know. On the opposite page, draw a picture of Jesus inside the heart wreath and give it to someone who needs to know that there is more to Easter than flowers and eggs.

And being found in appearance as a man,
he humbled himself and became obedient to death — even death on a cross! Philippians 2:8

Jesus Lives!

TO: _____

FROM: _____

This Easter, may you look to Jesus, who through His death and resurrection has given us the hope of life eternal. Praise be to God for His merciful grace and love!

Let us fix our eyes on Jesus, the author and perfecter of our faith, who for the joy set before him endured the cross, scorning its shame, and sat down at the right hand of the throne of God. Consider him who endured such opposition from sinful men, so that you will not grow weary and lose heart. Hebrews 12:2-3

Victory Over Death

On several occasions, Jesus told His disciples and friends that He would rise from the dead, but they forgot. The angel at the empty tomb reminded the women that Jesus rose from the dead just as He said He would. Sometimes as we celebrate Easter, we may also need to be reminded of Jesus' triumphant victory over death. On the opposite page, draw flowers at the foot of the cross and a heart in the center of the cross. Give the page to someone as a reminder of Jesus' resurrection.

The Son of Man must be delivered into the hands of sinful men, be crucified and on the third day be raised again. Then they remembered his words. Luke 24:7-8

TO: _____

FROM: _____

Wishing you Easter blessings as you celebrate the triumphant resurrection of Jesus Christ, our Lord and Savior.

For God so loved the world that he gave his one and only Son, that whoever believes in him shall not perish but have eternal life. John 3:16

Mother's Day

Even if your mother does not grow a garden, she is still growing something very precious according to God. She is growing you! Just like a gardener who makes sure her plants have the proper care, your mother sees that you get the proper care also. Can you think of some ways that your mother makes sure you grow up big and strong? Draw a picture of yourself on the inside of the flower on the opposite page and give the sheet to your mother.

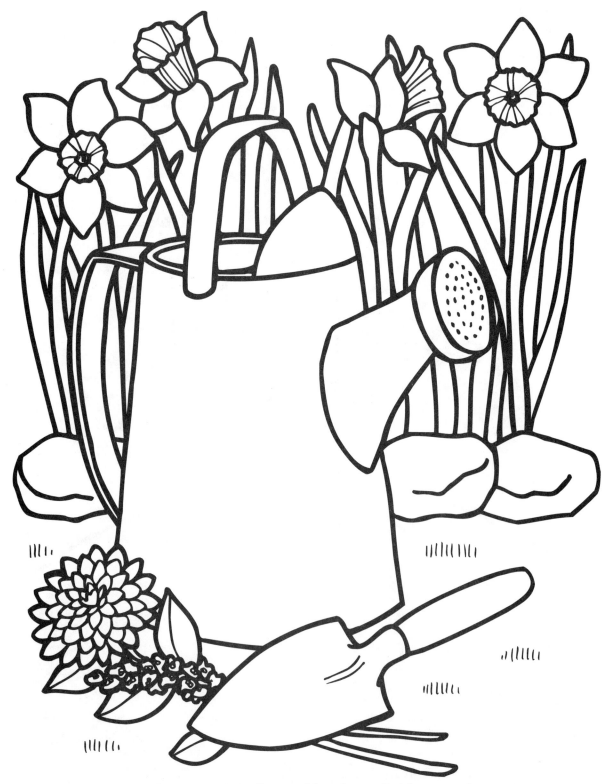

She watches over the affairs of her household. Proverbs 31:27

TO: _____

FROM: _____

I am like a flower
That is growing big and strong;
My loving home and family
Is the garden where I belong.

Your love and constant care for me
Is more than I could ask;
Growing a flower such as me
Is not an easy task.

Thank you, Mom,
for all you've done!
Happy Mother's Day
to the World's Best Gardener!

Her children arise and call her blessed. Proverbs 31:28

Mother's Arms

Have you ever been frightened by a terrible storm? Did your mother make you feel safe? Did she wrap you in her arms? Just being in your mother's arms is such a comfort at times when we need it. The Bible tells us that God is like a mother, too, who comforts us in our frightening moments. He protects us and keeps us safe. We need to thank our mothers for the protection and safety they give us. Draw a bouquet of flowers in the cat's hand on the opposite page. In the box, write a thank-you note to your mother for the protection she gives you.

As a mother comforts her child, so will I comfort you. Isaiah 66:13

TO: _____

FROM: _____

*Wishing you the
very best for Mother's Day!*

There is a time for everything…a time to love. Ecclesiastes 3:1,8

Father's Day

Have you ever gone hiking with people who led you through the mountain paths because they knew the way? Your father is like that. He can help you make the right decisions. Your father has a lot of wisdom to keep you from going on the wrong path if you listen. Our Heavenly Father will also guide us if we obey Him and follow His commands. On the opposite page, draw a picture of yourself in the frame and give the sheet to your father.

In all your ways acknowledge him, and he will make your paths straight. Proverbs 3:6

TO: _____

FROM: _____

I hope I make you proud of me
By the things I say and do;
And on this happy Father's Day
Comes a great big "I love you!"

Happy Father's Day from one
of your biggest fans!

Commit to the Lord whatever you do, and your plans will succeed. Proverbs 16:3

Father's Wisdom

Most Dads know how to do many things around the house, such as fix a leaky faucet or repair a broken window. Some fathers even built the house their family lives in. The Bible says that wisdom and understanding are what make a strong household. Wisdom and understanding come from knowing God and His Word.

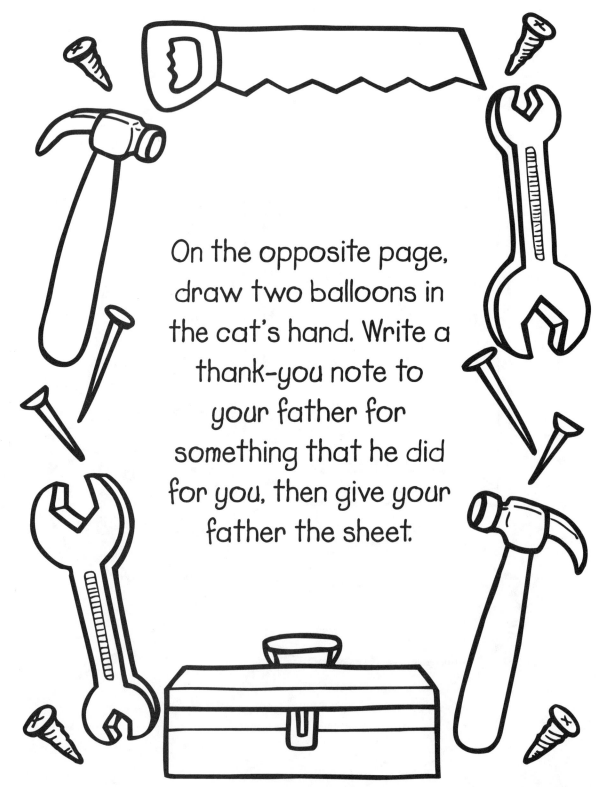

On the opposite page, draw two balloons in the cat's hand. Write a thank-you note to your father for something that he did for you, then give your father the sheet.

By wisdom a house is built, and through understanding it is established. Proverbs 24:3

TO: _____

FROM: _____

Wishing you the very best Father's Day for the very best father!

*Fathers, do not exasperate your children; instead,
bring them up in the training and instruction of the Lord.* Ephesians 6:4

Thanksgiving

Thanksgiving is the time of year when we remember how God has truly blessed this nation since its humble beginnings long ago. A faithful and dedicated group of Puritans took time to thank God for all that He had done for them. Can you think of something that someone gave you for which you are especially thankful to God? This would be a great time to thank someone with a card or note. Draw something that someone gave you for which you thank God inside the pumpkin on the opposite page.

Give thanks to the Lord, for he is good. His love endures forever. Psalm 136:1

TO: _____

FROM: _____

When I count my many blessings
Coming down from God above,
I thank Him for the kindness
You've showed to me in love.

Wishing you a Thanksgiving full of God's blessings!

And whatever you do, whether in word or deed, do it all in the name of the Lord Jesus,
giving thanks to God the Father through him. Colossians 3:17

Thanksgiving Care

Do you know people who could use a little cheering up during Thanksgiving? Maybe their family has all grown up and moved away and they will be alone for this holiday. Holidays are not always happy and joyous times for everyone. But you can make it brighter for others by letting them know you care about them. On the opposite page, draw more fruit in the basket and give the sheet to someone special.

The Lord will indeed give what is good, and our land will yield its harvest. Psalm 85:12

Thanksgiving Basket

TO: _____

FROM: _____

May God fill your life with His love and His blessings during Thanksgiving and all through the year.

Let us come before him with thanksgiving and extol him with music and song. Psalm 95:2

The Real Reason

Some Christmas cards say that Santa Claus, gifts and candy are what Christmas is all about. But Jesus is the real reason to celebrate Christmas. If you accept God's gift, you can have joy and hope. It is important that you share the hope of Jesus, especially during this time of year. Draw the baby Jesus in the manger on the opposite page and give it to someone who needs to know about Jesus.

Praise be to the Lord, the God of Israel,
because he has come and has redeemed his people. Luke 1:68

Jesus...The Greatest Gift Ever Given

May your Christmas be blessed with the hope, joy and peace that only Jesus can give.

To: _____

From: _____

For to us a child is born, to us a son is given. Isaiah 9:6

The Angel's Announcement

The good news of Jesus' birth was announced to the shepherds by an angel on the hillside of Bethlehem.

But the good news of Jesus is for all people everywhere.

Christmas is a time when we, like the angel, can tell others about God's Son, Jesus, who came to give us eternal life.

Draw a happy face on the angel on the opposite page and give it to someone who needs to hear the good news of Jesus' birth.

Today in the town of David a Savior has been born for you; he is Christ the Lord. Luke 2:11

TO: _____

FROM: _____

The angel announced
From heaven above:
A Savior is born –
God's gift of love.

May the angel's good news of long ago be a blessing to you this Christmas and throughout the year.

I bring you good news of great joy that will be for all the people. Luke 2:10

The Story of the Candy Cane

Do you know the meaning of the candy cane? The candy cane helps remind us what Christmas is all about — the life, death and resurrection of God's Son, Jesus. Be sure to read the story of the candy cane on the opposite page before giving it away. Draw the stripes on the candy cane on the opposite page and give it to someone who may not know the story of how the candy cane reminds us of the love and sacrifice of Jesus Christ.

By whose stripes ye were healed. 1 Peter 2:24 KJV

30

The Candy Cane Story

The candy cane has been a traditional holiday treat for many years. This simple Christmas decoration is full of symbolism that tells of the birth, ministry and death of our Lord and Savior Jesus Christ.

A candy maker wanted to use the candy cane to share the good news of Jesus Christ. So he made the candy cane pure white to symbolize the virgin birth and the sinless nature of Jesus. The hardness of the candy symbolizes the solid rock of Jesus Christ on which the church was founded and also the unwavering promises of God. The shape of the cane represents the staff of Jesus, our Good Shepherd, who guides us, His sheep, so we do not go astray. The cane also represents the staff of the shepherds who were the first to worship the newborn Christ. But most importantly, the cane when turned upside down is the letter "J" representing the precious name of Jesus.

The candy maker added red stripes to give it color. The large red stripes are symbolic of the blood of Jesus and the eternal life that we can have because of His death on the cross. The small stripes represent the beatings that Jesus received and the forgiveness we have as a result of His suffering.

Lastly, the candy maker gave the candy cane the flavor and aroma of peppermint, which is likened to the aromatic herb hyssop. In Bible times, hyssop was used for its savory taste and as a medicine.

The next time you see a candy cane, allow it to be a reminder to you of what Christmas is all about – Jesus, the only reason for the season.

With his stripes we are healed. Isaiah 53:5 KJV

Birthday Thoughts

God has given us so many things to be happy about. Growing up is one of them. We can thank God for giving us another year to do our best in serving Him. Jesus had birthdays, too, to mark His growing years. Do you think that Jesus' family celebrated His birthday? How does your family celebrate your birthday? Draw a hat on the clown on the opposite page and give it to someone who is having a birthday.

He seldom reflects on the days of his life,
because God keeps him occupied with gladness of heart. Ecclesiastes 5:20

TO: _____

FROM: _____

Wishing you
a fun-filled day
as you celebrate
another year that God
has given to you.

Happy Birthday!

This is the day the Lord has made; let us rejoice and be glad in it. Psalm 118:24

Let's Celebrate!

Every day of your life is a new day that God gives you. You should be happy for that very reason! Celebrating your birthday or someone else's birthday is another way you can thank God for guiding and protecting you in the past year and ask for His blessing in the coming year. On the opposite page, draw your favorite animals in the ark and give the sheet to someone who is celebrating a birthday.

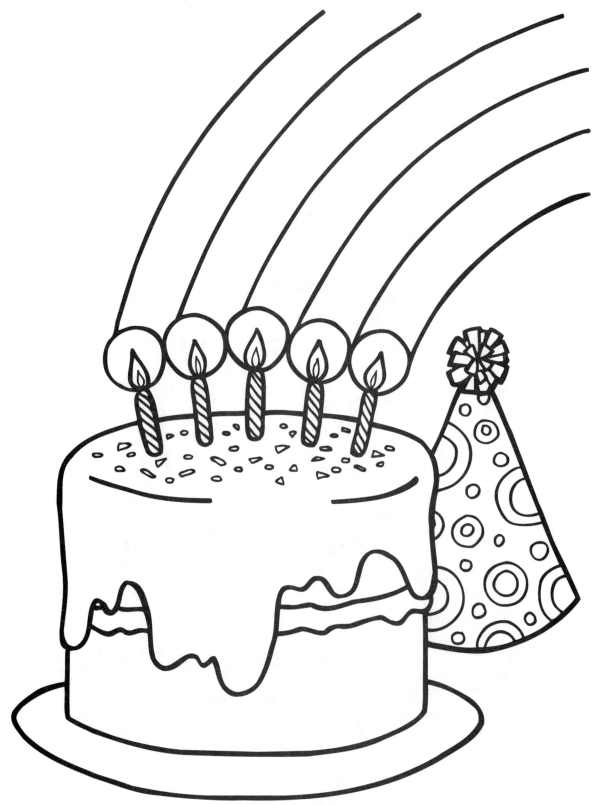

When times are good, be happy. Ecclesiastes 7:14

TO: _____

FROM: _____

These animals on Noah's Ark
Have come along your way
To wish for you the very best
On this, your Happy Birthday!

Happy Birthday!

Rejoice in the Lord always. Philippians 4:4

Giving Thanks

Has any one ever done something kind for you? Maybe your teacher encouraged you to do your very best. Or maybe you received a beautiful gift. How did it make you feel? When people do nice things for you, you should always remember to thank them. A nice way to thank someone is by writing a thank-you note. Think of someone you need to thank, then on the opposite page draw plants in the two pots and a sun shining through the window. Write in your own words why you thank the person and give the sheet to him or her.

Homework:
Math, pg 67, 1-25
Soc. Studies, pg

1. $\frac{3}{4} \times \frac{1}{2} =$

2. $\frac{1}{3} \times \frac{1}{3} =$

3. $\frac{1}{5} \times \frac{2}{3} =$

Be kind and compassionate to one another. Ephesians 4:32

TO: _____

FROM: _____

Thank you for the good things you have done for me!

Let us not become weary in doing good, for at the proper time
we will reap a harvest if we do not give up. Galatians 6:9

A Handful of Thanks

Jesus commanded us to love one another. We show our love by the way we treat each other and the good deeds we do. Have you ever picked a handful of flowers and given them to someone as a way of saying thank-you? You can also show your appreciation by writing to them. Is there someone to whom you can write a thank-you note? On the opposite page, draw a picture of yourself inside the heart wreath, write "From My Heart" on the banner and write for what you are thankful on the blank line.

A new command I give you: Love one another.
As I have loved you, so you must love one another. John 13:34

TO: _____

FROM: _____

I thank you with all my heart for _____.

Give thanks in all circumstances. 1 Thessalonians 5:18

Sick in Bed

You can pray for your sick friends so that they may get back to good health. You can also let them know that you are praying for and thinking of them. It makes people happy to know that someone cares for them when they are sick. On the opposite page, draw spots on the dog, write "Get Well" on the heart and give it to someone who is sick.

And the prayer offered in faith will make the sick person well. James 5:15

TO: _____

FROM: _____

Hoping and praying that you will
soon be back to good health!

Those who hope in the Lord will renew their strength. Isaiah 40:31

A Gift of Healing

Sometimes a serious illness causes people to turn to God and receive His gift of eternal life. When you pray for your sick friends, ask God to heal them and to change their hearts if they are not already Christians. You can send a note of hope as you pray for healing. Draw a bandage on the bear on the opposite page and a flower in his hand.

The God of all comfort, who comforts us in all our troubles, so that we can comfort those in any trouble with the comfort we ourselves have received from God. 2 Corinthians 1:3-4

TO: _____

FROM: _____

May you look to God our Father for your source of hope and strength as you recover from your illness.

For I am the Lord, your God, who takes hold of your right hand and says to you, Do not fear; I will help you. Isaiah 41:13

Wishes of Wellness

Have you ever received get-well cards when you were sick? It was encouraging to know that someone was thinking about you, wasn't it? Let's try to remember our friends and family members who may be recovering from surgery or an illness by cheering them up with a wish to get well soon! On the opposite page, draw heart-shaped cookies on the cookie sheet and give the page to someone who is ill.

For our light and momentary troubles are achieving for us
an eternal glory that far outweighs them all. 2 Corinthians 4:17

44

A Get-Well Recipe To: _____

From: _____

I'm baking up a Get-Well wish
That's made especially for you;
It's filled with many good things
To make you like brand-new!

I'm putting in lots of love,
And also lots of prayer,
With a dash of hugs and kisses
To show you that I care!

Hope you are feeling better soon!

Taste and see that the Lord is good; blessed is the man who takes refuge in him. Psalm 34:8

Thinking of You

Doing thoughtful things for people is a good way to let them know that you care about them. Sometimes you want to let others know that they are thought of in a special way. Draw some designs on the kites on the opposite page, write your name on the blank line and give it to someone who could use encouragement.

The Lord is my light and my salvation – whom shall I fear? Psalm 27:1

TO: _____

_____ **is thinking of you!**

Wishing you a day of joyful surprises!

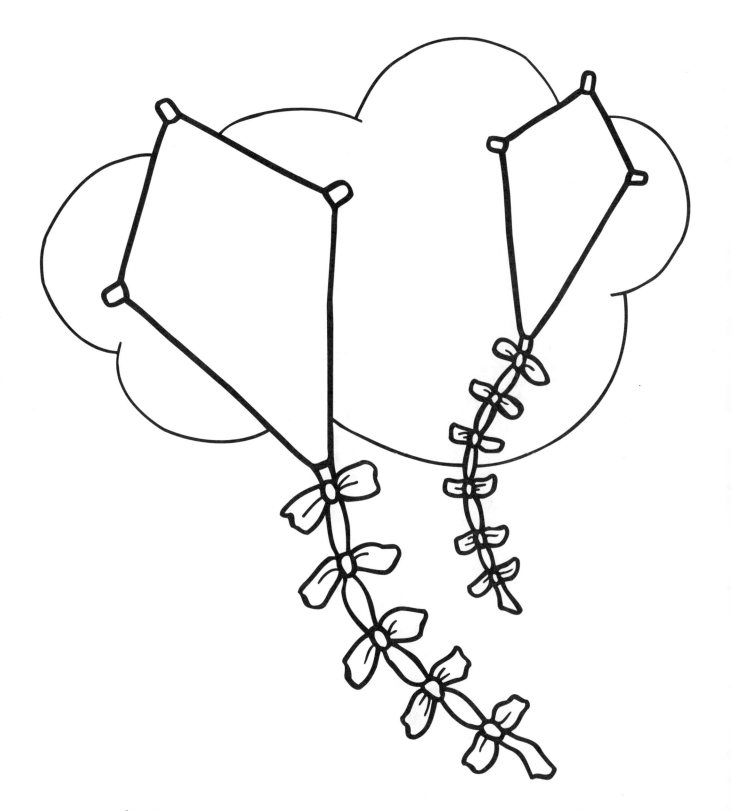

Wait for the Lord; be strong and take heart and wait for the Lord. Psalm 27:14

Good News

Do you like to receive mail? The Bible says when we receive good news from far away it will make us happy. We can make others happy, too, when we send them "good news" through the mail. Maybe a sick neighbor or an elderly shut-in could use some cheer. Draw flowers in the vase on the opposite page and give the sheet to the person who needs some good news.

Like cold water to a weary soul is good news from a distant land. Proverbs 25:25

To: _____

From: _____

Thinking of you this very day
And sending some cheer
along your way!

Therefore encourage one another and build each other up. 1 Thessalonians 5:11

Rejoice Always

There are some days when you may not be able to find many things to be happy about. When you are unhappy, you may tend to blame others or God. But God has given us much for rejoicing, such as His beautiful creation. On the opposite page, draw curtains and a picture of yourself in the window and give it to someone who may need to be reminded to rejoice in the Lord.

I will sing to the Lord all my life; I will sing praise to my God as long as I live. Psalm 104:33

TO: _____

FROM: _____

May God bless you in a special way today!

This is the day the Lord has made; let us rejoice and be glad in it. Psalm 118:24

An Invisible Gift

One of the best gifts you can give someone is invisible. It is the gift of prayer! When you pray for others you are presenting their concerns to your Heavenly Father. Are there those you know who need this invisible gift? You can give it to them any time, any day. On the opposite page, draw a face and hair on the child to make him or her look like you, then write your prayer in the bubble.

For you have been my hope, O Sovereign Lord, my confidence since my youth. Psalm 71:5

TO: _____

FROM: _____

I'm praying for you!

May God comfort you by His loving presence and fill your life with peace.

The prayer of a righteous man is powerful and effective. James 5:16

Trust God

When people go through hard times, such as a death in the family or the loss of a job, they will either draw closer to God for strength or they will blame God for the problems. Jesus promised us that He will never leave us. Are there those you know who may be having difficulty trusting in God for strength? You may let them know you are praying for them. On the opposite page, draw a design on the bedspread and a picture in the frame, then give the sheet to the person.

My times are in your hands; deliver me from
my enemies and from those who pursue me. Psalm 31:15

TO: _____

FROM: _____

To God our Father in the heavens
I'm sending up a heartfelt prayer;
That He will comfort and strengthen you
And keep you in His loving care!

You are in my prayers!

I call on you, O God, for you will answer me; give ear to me and hear my prayer. Psalm 17:6

You Are Missed

Are there a lot of children in your Sunday School class? We go to church to learn about God and His Son, Jesus. But sometimes we have to miss church because of sickness or another reason. Do you miss your friends when they are not in church? Let them know that you miss them so that they will be happy to come back. On the opposite page, draw a sun in the sky and faces on the flowers, then write the person's name in the empty heart and send it to him or her.

He said to them, "Let the little children come to me, and do not hinder them, for the kingdom of God belongs to such as these." Mark 10:14

TO: _____

FROM: _____

We miss you and hope to see you soon!

Continue in what you have learned…because you know those from whom you learned it.
2 Timothy 3:14-15

Praying for the World

Jesus instructed the disciples to go everywhere in the world to preach the good news. The good news is that Jesus paid the price for your sin. Because the disciples obeyed this "Great Commission" there are Christians all over the world today who are spreading the gospel. Missionaries need a lot of help to tell others about Jesus. You can help them do their work by giving them money and by praying for them. On the opposite page, write your prayer for a missionary whom you know and draw a few flowers and hearts. Then send the sheet to the missionary to show that you care.

Then the disciples went out and preached everywhere, and the Lord worked with them and confirmed his word by the signs that accompanied it. Mark 16:20

TO: _____

FROM: _____

My heart pours out to you in prayer.

May God bless you as you touch the lives of others with the love of Jesus!

And this is my prayer: that your love may abound more and more in knowledge and depth of insight, so that you may be able to discern what is best and may be pure and blameless until the day of Christ, filled with the fruit of righteousness that comes through Jesus Christ – to the glory and praise of God. Philippians 1:9-11

Children of the World

The good news is for all people of every race, nation and tribe. Did you know that there are children in the world who have never heard of Jesus? Missionaries go to foreign lands to teach the good news. You can help missionaries do their work by praying for them. What are some things that you could pray for? Have you ever thought about being a missionary some day? On the opposite page, draw hair to make the child look like you, draw a stuffed toy animal on the bed and write a prayer in the bubble. Send the sheet to a missionary.

Therefore go and make disciples of all nations, baptizing them in the name of the Father and of the Son and of the Holy Spirit, and teaching them to obey everything I have commanded you. And surely I am with you always, to the very end of the age. Matthew 28:19-20

TO: _____

FROM: _____

I'm praying for you!

Whatever you do, whether in word or deed, do it all in the name of the Lord Jesus, giving thanks to God the Father through him. Colossians 3:16-17

Missionary Mission

You can support a missionary in a foreign land in many ways. Writing letters is one method, because most missionaries get little mail from home. Sending money is another way to help, but keeping them in your prayers is the most important. On the opposite page, draw pictures of missionaries inside the frames. Then write on the lines beside each photo who the person is and how you will pray for him or her. Keep this sheet at your bedside to remind you to pray for these people every night.

Serve one another in love. Galatians 5:13

My Prayer Reminder

I will remember to pray for:

1. _____
_____
_____
_____
_____
_____

2. _____
_____
_____
_____
_____
_____

3. _____
_____
_____
_____
_____
_____

Night and day I constantly remember you in my prayers. 2 Timothy 1:3